IMAGES OF ENGLAND

AYLESBURY

IMAGES OF ENGLAND

AYLESBURY

COLIN J. SEABRIGHT

TEMPUS

Frontispiece: The bottom of Market Square looking past the
Greyhound Hotel, photographed from Great Western Street around
1915.

First published 2006

Tempus Publishing Limited
The Mill, Brimscombe Port,
Stroud, Gloucestershire, GL5 2QG
www.tempus-publishing.com

© Colin J. Seabright, 2006

British Library Cataloguing in Publication Data.
A catalogue record for this book is available from the British Library.

ISBN 0 7524 3818 2

Typesetting and origination by Tempus Publishing Limited.
Printed in Great Britain.

Contents

In this 1908 view of part of Park Street, all the children from the terraced houses have come out on to the pavement to pose for the camera.

Acknowledgements

The illustrations, mostly postcards, are all from my own collection of Buckinghamshire ephemera, and, due to their age, I believe them to be out of commercial copyright; if not, I apologise for any infringement.

I must thank all the original photographers and publishers, both local and national, who produced the cards, those who first bought and sent them and the recipients who kept them for several decades, eventually passing them on to the card dealers from whom I have been lucky enough to purchase them.

Introduction

To quote from a 1949 school geography book:

> Aylesbury's history is a long one, for Saxon legends of the Manor of Aylesbury still remain. The first charter granting the town an annual fair dates from the time of Henry III, while the name of Kingsbury witnesses to the time when Aylesbury was itself a royal manor, and marks the king's holding when he eventually granted the manor to one of his nobles.

This is not the place to go into the detail of Aylesbury's long history, simply to provide a brief introduction to the pictures, selected to illustrate some features of the town as it was, from Victoria's time to the middle of the twentieth century. Aylesbury was still only a medium sized market town when, in 1725, it became the county town of Bucks, in which it is more or less central, in place of Buckingham at the extreme northern end of the county. It owed its prosperity to its position in the Vale of Aylesbury, some of the richest pasture-land in the country, and to the market that sold its produce.

A county guide published in 1805 noted:

> The town centre consists of several irregular streets and lanes; and according to the returns made under the Population Act in 1801, then contained 697 houses, and 3,082 inhabitants. Since Leland wrote of the town in the sixteenth century as well built of timber, the town has been very much improved, and most of the houses are now of brick. The improvements were principally owing to the munificence of Sir John Baldwin, chief justice in the reign of Henry VIII, who, at his own expence erected several public buildings, and procured the assizes to be held here instead of Buckingham. The county gaol is still in Aylesbury, but the summer assizes were, in the year 1758, restored to Buckingham. The town of Aylesbury has had from time immemorial a considerable market, the tolls of which in the reign of Edward the Confessor were valued at £25 per annum. The present market, which is held on Saturday, was granted by charter of Queen Elizabeth, dated 1579. There is no manufacture in the town, and the principal business is lace-making. Aylesbury was made a borough town by a charter of Queen Mary, in 1554, and the parish, including the hamlet of Walcot [Walton], is the largest and most fertile in the county.

Hand lace-making soon died out, due to competition from the new machine-made lace, but the market and the town flourished. At the end of the nineteenth century, when Aylesbury's population had grown to 10,000, county guides noted:

> Although Aylesbury has been largely modernised, especially in respect to its public buildings, there are a good many private houses of considerable antiquity, and many of the streets retain their pristine narrowness. The most interesting of the town's buildings is the King's Head Inn, a

beautiful timbered hostelry, standing a little way up an alley on the westerly side of the Market Place. The Market Place itself contains little that is ancient. It is a wide square on a considerable slope, paved with granite sets, partly fenced off by iron railings for the holding of cattle markets. In the centre is an elaborate modern Clock Tower. In the High Street are one or two timbered houses, but their fronts, at all events, are quite modern.

and:

Aylesbury's paved cattle market, second to none in any provincial town, where a weekly sale of fat and store stock is held on Wednesday, as is also, in the Market Square, a market for store cattle and sheep on Saturdays, the statutory market day.

A few years later, when the population had reached 12,000, a local guide was enthusiastic about the town's facilities:

Aylesbury is a very good model of what a country-town should be. It is clean and self-respecting, but not aggressively so. Its inhabitants are, for the most part, neither very poor nor over rich. Its public buildings are good, and it is animated by a progressive spirit, yet it contains enough of the old and the picturesque to prove its long lineage. The traveller desiring to come to Aylesbury, be he bent on pleasure or business, has plenty of scope for the exercise of taste and the study of convenience. Perhaps there is no town of its size, and of equal distance from London, that possesses so excellent a train service. The London & North Western, Great Western, Metropolitan, and Great Central Railways all offer their own particular advantages, the result being a variety of routes and a daily service of trains that leave nothing to be desired.

Growth continued without any major changes, and after the Second World War, with a population of 21,000, the town was recognised not only as a market centre, but also as a place worth visiting for its own sake and its attractive setting:

Situated in the Vale of Aylesbury in one of the most beautiful parts of Buckinghamshire, of which it is the county town, Aylesbury stands on high ground formed of Portland rock and is some 300ft above sea level at its highest point. It forms an admirable centre for walking and motoring tours and is 40 miles from London via Wendover, Amersham and Uxbridge, or 38 miles via Tring, Berkhamsted and Watford. Aylesbury is an important and thriving market centre with a picturesque market square and many interesting old buildings and is within easy reach of all parts of the Chilterns as excellent bus services run to all the surrounding villages.

Then, in the late fifties and sixties, when the population had reached 32,000 the blight of development and 'improvement' hit the town badly, and although most of the High Street and Kingsbury escaped, the south-west side of Market Square, and many of Aylesbury's oldest and most interesting back streets between it and the railway, were demolished by a council hell-bent on 'modernising' the shopping facilities making the shopping centre a carbon copy of hundreds of other such centres with all the same multiple stores in concrete buildings, all overlooked by a monstrous tower block of council offices.

The pictures in this book show, in the first section, parts of Aylesbury at the end of the Victorian era, then subsequent sections illustrate various features during the first half of the twentieth century, before the modern developments completely spoilt the town.

Limitations of space prevent more than a brief coverage of those features, and I am sorry if your favourite building or street scene could not be included.

Colin J. Seabright
January 2006

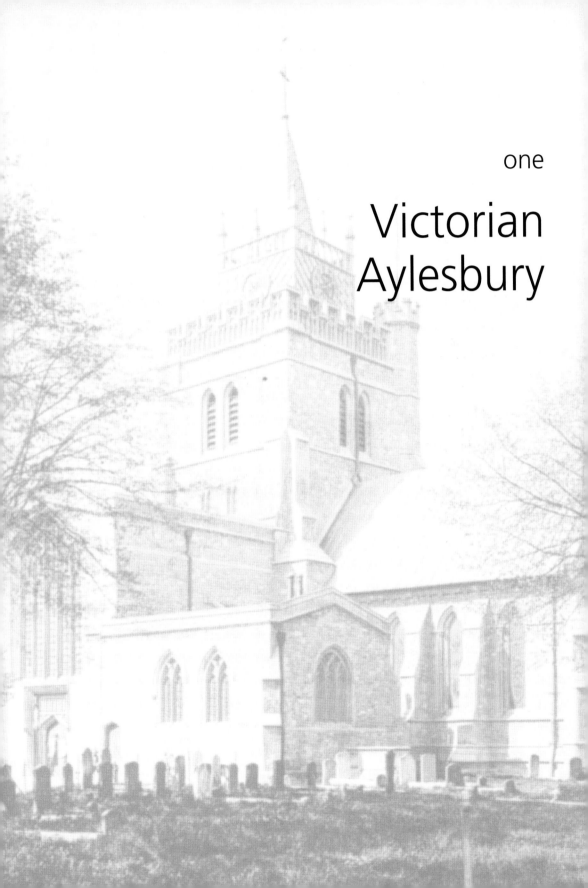

one

Victorian
Aylesbury

The Aylesbury Market Co.'s new Corn Exchange was ceremonially opened on 11 October 1865, and this sketch of the crowds attending the event was published in the *Illustrated London News* ten days later. The building, on the site of the historic White Hart Hotel, extended further to the left out of view, and included a large Market Hall. The company's offices occupied the rooms over the arches, and their hall, reached from inside the arches, was also used for concerts, charity bazaars, etc., and was the venue for the town's first occasional cinema shows in 1899.

A view down the empty Market Square in the 1870s. This was after the demolition of the 1806 Market House which had stood in the middle of the square, but before construction of the Clock Tower there. The irregular shape of the 'square' is due to later buildings encroaching on its sixteenth-century layout, hiding some of the earliest hostelries, etc., which lined the original perimeter.

Published as a postcard in 1900, this photograph of the top corner of Market Square was taken around five years earlier. Although many people were pictured walking or standing around, only one market stall can be seen, outside the cobbled area; on the corner in front of the Crown Hotel, beside the entrance to High Street.

Above: This view of the entrance to Aylesbury by the Hartwell Road was photographed by a visitor to the town in September 1875. Faintly visible, straight ahead through the haze, houses cover the hillside below the church. The bridge in the centre of the photograph carries the road over the tail-race of Aylesbury Mill.

Left: High Street was developed in 1826 as a direct link from Market Square to the Tring Road. Mainly residential, it was known as New Road until around 1890, when, with shop fronts added to some of the houses, it gradually began to take its place as a commercial centre. Here, the top end, where it curves into Market Square, was photographed in 1880 from an upper window of S.G. Payne's studio on the corner of Britannia Street.

This page: These 1880s views of the town's most significant buildings are more examples of the work of S.G. Payne. The Corn Exchange (above left), was the property of the Aylesbury Market Co.; its archway led to the open-air livestock market. County Hall (above right), built between 1720 and 1740, included court rooms and judges' lodgings, as well as the County Council Chamber and principal offices. St Mary's, the parish church (right), is pictured behind the rough grass of the churchyard, framed between mature trees that still contribute to the beauty of its setting.

Kingsbury originally formed one continuous open space with Market Square until encroachment near the entrance to Cambridge Street effectively separated the two areas. The Town Pump, behind the group of children on the right in this 1890 photograph, supplied all the water to the area from 1838 to 1894.

Right: This 1890 amateur photograph from an upper window of the Queen's Head public house in Temple Square shows the south-east side of that square. The three-storey building included the grocery shop of bacon curer Richard Thorp, whose business continued until the Second World War.

Below: Completion, in 1815, of the Aylesbury Arm of the Grand Union Canal (a six-mile branch down from Marsworth) was a great boost to the town, providing cheap, if rather slow, transport for heavy goods to and from both London and the Midlands. It greatly reduced the price of coal in the town. The 1897 photograph, from the towpath looking over Park Street toward the town, includes the lowest of the twelve locks of the canal.

Aylesbury Canal and Lock.

Opposite below: Much of the town was decorated for the celebrations to mark Queen Victoria's Diamond Jubilee in 1887. In Kingsbury, flags and banners cover the frontage of wine merchants Gulliver & Co. and most of the neighbouring buildings, including The Eagle, a few doors along. Decorations at the top of the area can be seen through the triumphal arches, below which straw was laid on the roadway.

This view, looking up Market Square from the Corn Exchange corner, was published in *The Royal Souvenir Album of the Vale of Aylesbury* by Ancient & Armstrong, stationers, of Market Square, around 1890. The stylised picture includes the shops of William Rowe, ironmonger, and Harry Mitchell, butcher, in the block of buildings which extends onto the original square.

Another late Victorian view up the market, this one from an upper window of County Hall and published by Samuel Payne, shows the extent of the empty cobbled area below the Clock Tower, with a market in progress beyond it. The extreme right-hand shop, under the end three blinds, was then Kingham & Sons' high-class provision store, including their Floral Hall.

two

Transport

Canal, Aylesbury.

Above and below: Here, in the 1920s, a narrow-boat is being manually hauled past Coronation Villas on the last stretch of the canal into Aylesbury Basin. Being at the bottom of a series of locks, all the extra water let through with each boat often caused the basin to overflow and flood the nearby streets. The covered wharf was at the extreme end of the canal, which almost reached Walton Street, from where this 1961 photograph was taken. As commercial traffic dwindled, the wide part of the canal basin, behind this building, became home to a number of house-boats.

Above and below: Aylesbury's first railway, and Britain's first branch line, was the seven-mile link opened in 1839 between the town and Cheddington on the London & North Western Railway's London to Birmingham main line, which brought Aylesbury within reasonable reach of the capital. The route entered the town beside the road known as Stock Lake, pictured from the foot-bridge over the line at Park Street. Thirty years after the line opened, its terminus was moved from Station Street to a new site beside the gas-works on High Street. Although the line carried much goods traffic, it was never very popular with passengers, who preferred the later, more direct, Metropolitan & Great Central route to London from Aylesbury Town station. This view of the old High Street station, which closed in 1953, dates from its last day of service.

The GWR reached Aylesbury, via Princes Risborough, in 1863. In 1892 the Metropolitan Railway also reached the town, sharing the same station, and was joined in 1899 by the Great Central on its new

main line to the Midlands. This view of the joint station was photographed from the footbridge early in the twentieth century.

At Christmas 1904 a dreadful accident occurred, when a parcel train ploughed into a de-railed newspaper train at the eastern end of the station, killing four railway employees. Here, a few days later, the maintenance gangs are still restoring the tracks, watched by a couple on the repaired platform.

Officially named Aylesbury Town, the joint station was connected directly to the town centre by Great Western Street. The station building is pictured in the twenties, with a cattle dock on the left beside the forecourt entrance.

Above: A Metropolitan Train is seen here picking up a barrow-load of papers before departing for Verney Junction in the 1930s. The footbridge, partly visible through the steam and smoke from the engine, carries the public path linking California with the rest of the town.

Left: This hand-propelled tricycle was specially made locally for its rider Jimmy Goodwin, who had lost the use of his legs as a child. He was a regular and popular feature of Market Square, selling boxes of matches to the farmers and stall-holders and their visitors, from the early 1900s (when this photo was taken) until the 1920s.

Left and below: The Walton Engine Works was established around 1870 by John Fraser, general engineer and agricultural implement maker. Twenty years later it was run by William Morris, trading also as iron and brass founder, who had a narrow-gauge railway around the yard of the works in Walton Road, for the conveyance of heavy castings between buildings. Regularly, from 1906 to 1914, S.G. Payne photographed his friends riding around the works and adjoining garden on trucks drawn by a smart steam engine.

A smartly turned out pony and trap conveys members of the Goodson family away from their home at Dunsham Farm, around 1900, with other members of the household watching from the doorway.

In the 1900s the horse was still the most common form of propulsion for local transport, both for people and goods. Here a horse-drawn chaise overtakes a handcart at the entrance to Kingsbury, where several carts are parked in the centre.

Even after motor vehicles became readily available, horse-drawn carts remained popular for local delivery rounds, because the horses grew to know their regular routes and stopping points as well as their drivers did, and needed very little instruction. Here, in 1908, Harry Saunders of Cambridge Street has stopped outside Arthur Luck's photographic studio to deliver the day's fish fresh from the coast to houses in Park Street.

A novel form of transport has been found for these two youngsters. The fair baby is 'little Mabel', according to 'Tot', the writer of this postcard in November 1906.

Right: Advertising, in 1907, for the Aylesbury Carriage Works who made and repaired bodies for both motor cars and horse-drawn vehicles. Buying and selling second-hand vehicles, they were among the earliest used-car dealers.

Below: The popularity of the motorcar immediately gave rise to a need for parking places and in the early twenties cars took over Market Square, parking randomly on the cobbles when not used by the market stalls. They also filled every available corner, including the centre of Temple Square, later officially recognised as a parking place for four cars.

Temple Square, Aylesbury

Another local operator, Red Rover Coaches, joined them in the thirties and opened an office in Kingsbury. Other, more distant companies, including Thames Valley and City of Oxford, also extended routes to Aylesbury, using Kingsbury as their terminus.

Opposite above and below: Ernest Young, proprietor of the County Garage in Buckingham Street, started Aylesbury's first motorised bus service, to Wendover, soon after the First World War. Services grew rapidly and school children are seen here boarding one of his buses bearing Aylesbury Borough licence number 15. By 1922 Ernest Young's Aylesbury Motor Bus Co. was operating routes to Princes Risborough, Thame, Waddesdon, Leighton Buzzard and Berkhamsted, though some ran on market days only. They used Kingsbury as a terminus, where the triangular central island made a convenient bus stand.

Kingsbury was officially recognised as a bus station by 1938 when the council built a permanent shelter on the island. Bus stops, with railings for the queues, were also installed and allocated to specific routes. By this time the Aylesbury Bus Co. had been taken over by Eastern National.

By 1950 some of the main routes were served by double-deckers, mostly belonging to the major operators: London Transport; United Counties; Thames Valley; City of Oxford and Eastern National but Red Rover was still running many of the local routes.

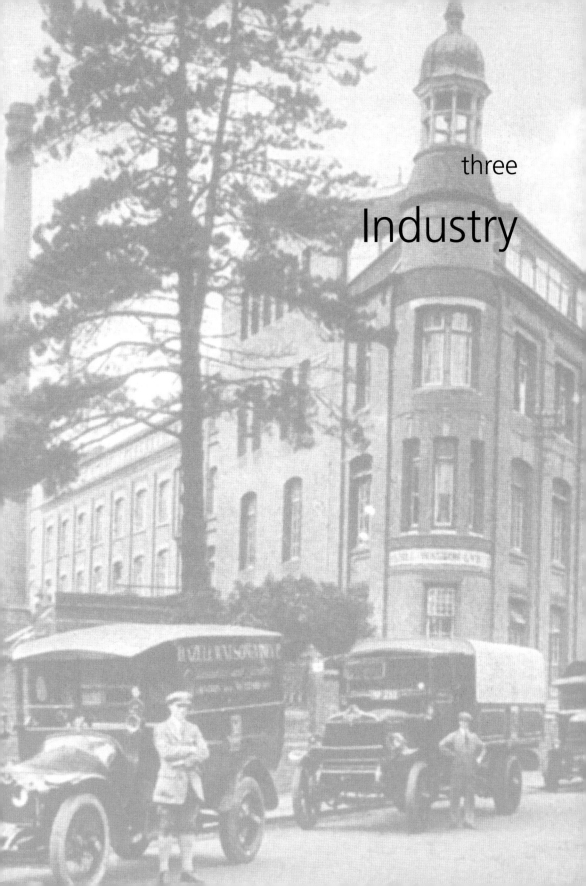

three

Industry

WALTON POND

The Aylesbury Duck is a distinct breed, always white with a pale pink beak and orange feet. Its offspring grow rapidly, reaching table-ready size in about eight weeks, and were highly regarded by Mrs Beeton. For most of the nineteenth century vast quantities were bred locally for the London market, many by small breeders as a second occupation. To get them through their first few weeks, the delicate ducklings were handreared in the homes of their owners, shared their living and bedrooms and later allowed out to paddle in the nearest available pond or stream. Pictured around 1900, ducks from several local broods swim happily together on Walton Pond.

Above and below: Many of the small-scale duck breeders lived in the area of White Hill and the Oxford Road, which became known locally as Duck End. Here, in 1910, Oxford Road is seen across the meadow and the mill-stream, the duck's nearest stretch of water. In the twentieth century the small duckbreeders in the town slowly gave up, though ducks were still to be found in surrounding villages, particularly in Weston Turville. A few larger duck farms survived, though the last of these closed in the late fifties.

The Aylesbury Gas Co. was formed in 1834 and almost immediately supplied gas from their works to lamps in all the main streets. Known later as the Gaslight & Coke Co., the works were next door to the LNWR station, with sidings for direct delivery of coal into their yard. On this 1910 view up High Street the gas-holder overshadows the station roof.

William Ingram established his business as nurseryman and seedsman around 1860 at 'The Vine Nursery' in Wendover Road, Walton. Joined by a partner, around 1890 the firm became Ingram, Whitfield & Co., nurserymen and florists, and at the end of the nineteenth century the premises were re-named Walton Nurseries. This 1910 postcard shows the Wendover Road house closely surrounded by greenhouses that also stretched well back toward the railway.

Above and below: London printers Hazell & Watson opened a country branch in a former silk mill at California, behind the GWR station, in 1867. Joined by a third partner from an influential Aylesbury family, they moved in May 1878, and continued as Hazell, Watson & Viney, to a large new factory adjacent to the cemetery in Tring Road. Continuous expansion included, in 1895, a single-storey machine room on the Tring Road frontage, seen in the upper, 1900 view. The lower view, from the mid-1920s, shows how much further building had developed, with the manager's house in the foreground.

Around 1910, small deliveries from the printing works were made by pony and trap.

Hazell, Watson & Viney bought a small fleet of ex-army vans in 1922. Three of these, a Crossley, a Dennis, and an AEC, together with an Atkinson steam lorry, are pictured in Tring Road in 1924.

Fire precautions were essential in a plant with so much paper around, and from the early days the printers employed their own fire brigade. They are seen here in the twenties at the gates of the company's additional site on the opposite side of Tring Road.

USE **MILKMAID**
COFFEE
AND
MILK

UNEQUALLED.

Extremely convenient for **Travellers, Tourists,**
picnics, yachts, etc., as well as for household use. **A cup of coffee in one minute—**
only boiling water required.

MANUFACTURED AT AYLESBURY.

Left: The Anglo-Swiss Condensed Milk Co., in
association with Nestlé, established their milk-
processing plant at Aylesbury in 1870, where they
could take advantage of the ample supply of milk
from the rich pastureland surrounding the town.
They also made good use of the transport facilities
by canal and by rail to distribute their output.
As well as Nestlé's condensed milk and Ideal
evaporated milk, they produced other lines under
their Milkmaid brand name, as local advertising
from 1907 shows.

Below: This 1908 view of the milk-processing
factory, in the angle between lower High Street and
Park Road, includes the vast extensions built not
long after the original works, which are at the far
end, in front of the chimney.

The milk-processing plant raised steam daily at 6.00 a.m. and an hour later the gates were opened for the local farmers, who had been queueing in High Street, to deliver their milk. This photograph, from the town directory of 1922, shows the procession of assorted farm carts on the entrance road, all with their churns of fresh milk.

The factory had a long frontage to the canal, where two wharves allowed narrow-boats to load boxes of tins from a chute directly from inside the works. Canal transport, though slow, was ideal for this type of product: heavy and not immediately perishable.

Left: Samuel Glendenning Payne, Aylesbury's most prolific early photographer, worked from his High Street studio from around 1875 (when the address was still New Road) until the First World War in partnership with his wife, and, later, his son. This decorative advertisement was printed on the back of an 1885 cabinet photograph. Their offer of life-size enlargements would prove difficult in this case, as the subject was St Mary's church.

Below: After the Aylesbury Market Co. went out of business, T. Loader used the building behind the Corn Exchange as a warehouse for corn and oil-cake, from which they supplied the farmers attending the adjacent livestock market. Advertising their specialities – agricultural seeds and fertilizers – they continued in business until the 1960s.

Above: Agriculture remained the principal industry of the Aylesbury district in the first quarter of the twentieth century. This photograph of a horse-drawn reaper dates from 1916, when all the younger men had been called up for military service, leaving their older colleagues and the women to run the farms.

Right: Hunt, Barnard & Co., another London printers, followed Hazell & Watson's example and opened a major factory in Aylesbury in 1898, installing their machinery in The Granville Works - a ten-year-old building in Buckingham Street, which had been built as a model steam bakery. This picture is a 1907 advertisement for the company.

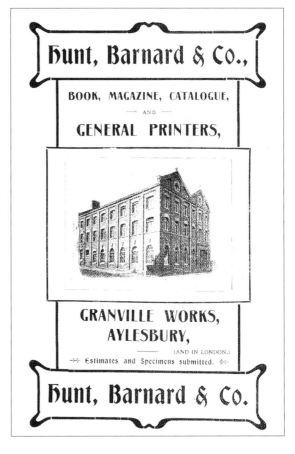

Hunt, Barnard & Co.,

BOOK, MAGAZINE, CATALOGUE,

— AND —

GENERAL PRINTERS,

**GRANVILLE WORKS,
AYLESBURY,**

(AND IN LONDON.)

⁘ Estimates and Specimens submitted. ⁘

Hunt, Barnard & Co.

Presumably to help their clients to recognise the agent standing on the doorstep, the Prudential Insurance Co. issued this card in 1907. The Aylesbury District superintendent, Albert James Merry, and his wife are seated in the centre of the small group.

BIFURCATED RIVET WORKS, AYLESBURY

One of Aylesbury's oldest established engineering firms, the Bifurcated & Tubular Rivet Co. built this factory in Mandeville Road in 1910. The factory's steam hooter, which could be heard several miles away, was regarded as the whole town's alarm clock, and was also used to call out the volunteer firemen.

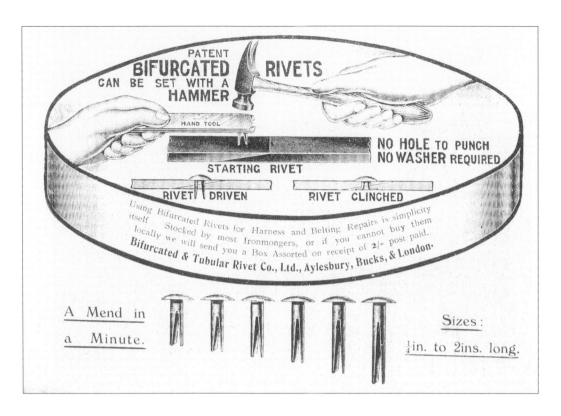

Above: The factory's main product was their patented bifurcated rivets; this 1922 advertisement shows how to use them to affect a quick and easy repair to leather belting without special tools.

Right: For a few years after the First World War, during which a part of the factory had been taken over as a military hospital, the Iris car was manufactured in the works, and seen here also in an advertisement from 1922.

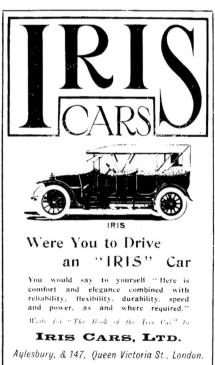

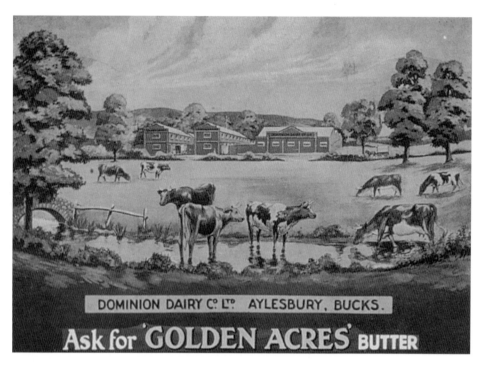

DOMINION DAIRY C° L™ AYLESBURY, BUCKS.

Ask for 'GOLDEN ACRES' BUTTER

In 1911 Dominion Dairy opened their milk-processing plant in Aylesbury, where they produced butter and, later, cheese, which was mostly despatched by rail for speedy delivery. This advertising postcard for their Golden Acres Butter is an artist's idealistic image of the factory, surrounded by golden acres, whereas, in reality, it was at the edge of the town, in Bicester Road.

This DELIGHTFUL COTTAGE MAY BE YOURS!

Purchase a Packet Now of Chilvern Cottage Cheese for full Details and Entry Form for Contest No. 2

To Improve Your fortunes buy Packets not Portions

Six freehold Cottages fully furnished, value £1,750 each, are the awards!

Advertising campaigns with large giveaways are nothing new; this cottage was the ultimate prize in a competition entered by purchasing Chilvern Cottage Cheese in the early thirties.

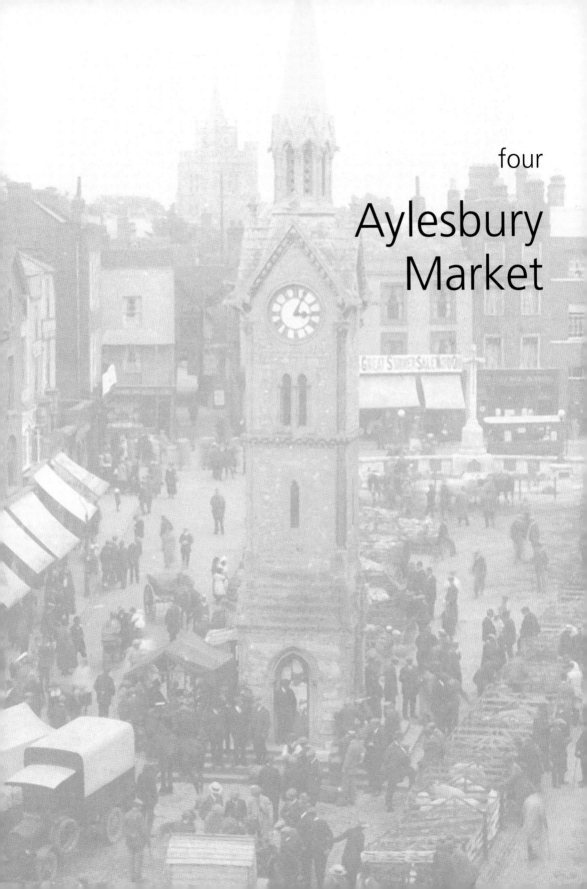

four

Aylesbury
Market

Above and below: Around 1900 a directory noted that Aylesbury Market, held every Saturday, was abundantly supplied with meat, grain, cattle, pigs, poultry and other agricultural produce and was very well attended. Sales of fatstock were also held on Wednesdays. These two postcards from the turn of the twentieth century show the well-attended market with straw laid on the cobbles for the animals, and a line of cattle waiting patiently for sale.

The Cattle Market, Aylesbury.

Above: Many cattle were also sold in the main livestock market behind County Hall, pictured in about 1910.

Next page: Here, on a Saturday morning in about 1905, sheep are penned ready for sale near the top of Market Square, ignored by the bowler-hatted gents passing by on their way to work. When the market was over for the day the Volunteer Fire Brigade was called in to hose down the cobbles.

The official livestock market, run by the council following the demise of the Aylesbury Market Co., had the advantage of direct access from Exchange Street, avoiding the congestion in Market Square. Pictured in 1910, it drew crowds of farmers and onlookers. The council charged standard tolls for the use of the market, for example 1s per stallion, 6d per bull, 2d per cow, 1d per calf, and 10d per score of sheep, lambs or pigs.

Opposite above: In addition to the regular twice-weekly markets, specialist fairs were held on six Saturdays in the year. Here, at a horse fair around 1910, the animals are lined up for inspection in the road outside the Bell Hotel.

Opposite below: After around 1910, the sale of animals in Market Square dwindled as more farmers made use of the official livestock market which offered much easier access for the delivery and collection of animals.

AYLESBURY.

Top of Market Square, shewing John Hampden Memorial.

This mixed market in the square in the mid-1920s was one of the last before all animal sales were transferred to the separate livestock market in 1927.

The Market, Aylesbury

Previously confined to the area below the Clock Tower, from 1927 the general stall market was given access to the whole area of Market Square, and on a postcard used in 1931 stallholders have taken full advantage of this freedom. The daily charges for such use of the cobbled area were: 10s per two-wheeled cart and 15s per van, when used for display or selling, or 1s per small (six feet) stall plus 3d for each cart left standing in the square.

Some of the stalls on a fine sunny market day in the mid-1930s.

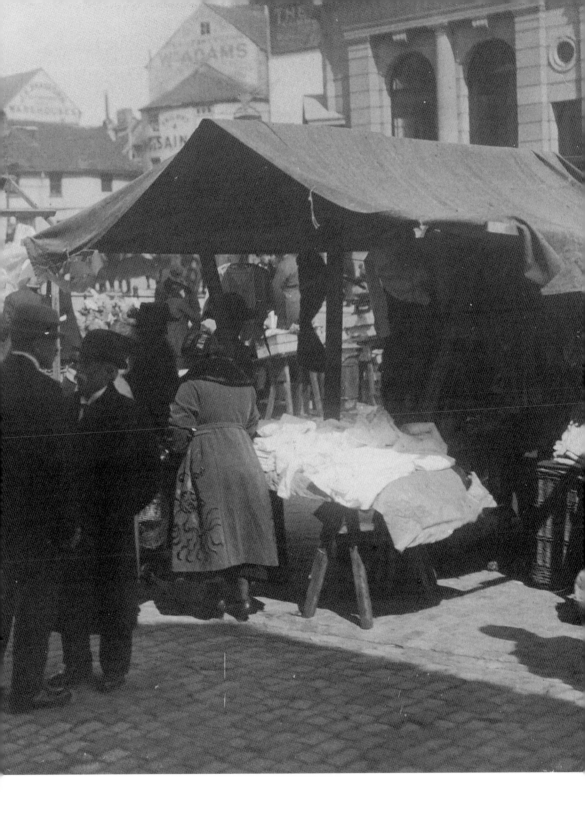

Some idea of the extent of the general market can be gained from this 1940s rooftop view over the covered stalls packed tightly within the railed-in area of the square. Approximately a hundred separate stalls can be seen, with more out of view at the bottom of the picture.

This view of the top of Market Square was photographed by a student at RAF Halton and published in their college magazine in 1953. Some of the busy stalls can hardly be seen, hidden behind swarms of potential customers.

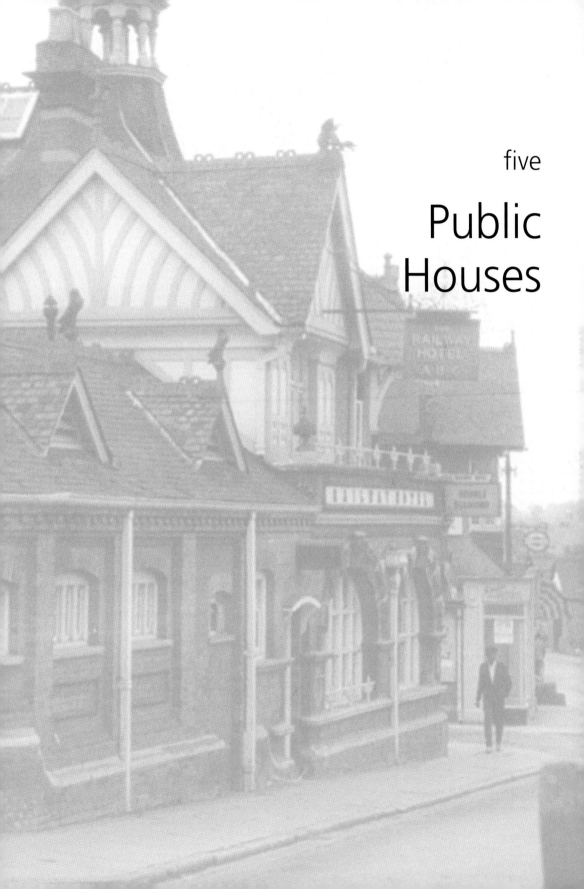

five

Public
Houses

Above and below: The King's Head, Aylesbury's oldest and most famous hostelry, dates from the fifteenth century and was patronised by Henry VIII. When first built the front windows faced directly onto Market Square, but the buildings to the right in the upper, 1910, view were later encroachments on to the square in front of the inn. The lower picture, of the hall, once described as a fine example of medieval architecture, shows its famous window, which includes much original glass in the heavy oak frames.

For the first time in 300 years the frontage of the Kings Head was for time open to view from Market Square, following the 1962 demolition of the shop building directly in front of it, and before construction of its replacement.

Facing down Market Square, the George Hotel, which had been re-fronted in 1827, was described in a 1907 guide as 'a capital hostelry, comfortable and reasonable, with old associations and features, but modern facilities'. Seen on the left in this 1915 view from a high window on the west side of the square, it was run by Thomas Seaton in conjunction with the wine merchants next door and the Angel Hotel in Kingsbury. He was also proprietor of the Aylesbury Steeplechase Course at Southcourt.

Above: Pictured on their advertising postcard from around 1905, the Crown Hotel, at the top of Market Square, had been severely reduced in size when New Road was created beside it. Described in 1928 as 'an exceedingly comfortable hostelry with old beam floors and ancient fireplaces', it was demolished in 1937.

Left: One of two temperance hotels in Market Square, this picture of Frederick Batchelor's The Vale comes from a 1912 advertisement that noted their specialities: Tea, Coffee, Cocoa, Chops and Steaks. Offering home comforts at moderate charges (a daily charge of 1s 6d per single room), this commercial and cyclists' hotel boasted a dining room upstairs, with hot dinners and teas provided on Sundays.

Right and below: Only slightly younger than the King's Head, the Bull's Head Hotel, also partly hidden from Market Square by later encroachment, was a very popular hostelry, particularly because of its jovial owner from 1910 onwards, Giacomo Gargini, who was elected mayor in the thirties. It is pictured (above) before it was given the moch-Tudor façade in 1920, and (below) with timbering as it is best remembered.

The sender of this card noted that they had had an excellent lunch in the heavily beamed and panelled dining room of the Bull's Head

The Bell Hotel, also in Market Square, is pictured well before the 1919 restoration and extension which completely changed its appearance. The alterations added an extra storey overall, and more accommodation behind the original building, which was given a new, angled entrance on the Walton Street corner and a frontage of rendered panels between columns of exposed brickwork.

The focus of a network of narrow alleyways, created by the later medieval buildings on the south side of Market Square, was the sixteenth century Dark Lantern Inn. Pictured in 1950, it was given a little more breathing space when most of its neighbours were demolished for the 1960s redevelopment of the area.

The White Horse Inn, one of nearly a dozen licensed premises around Market Square, closed in 1925. After a few short-term occupiers, the old building, on a sloping site at the edge of the square, opened in the mid-1930s as the Old Beams tea room.

Above and left: Though beams are not much in evidence in the above view of the Old Beams restaurant's interior, the whole building was supported on massive timbers over a sunken passageway from Market Square to Silver Lane, which was sketched by M. M. Lloyd in the lower postcard.

Near Market Square,
Aylesbury.

M M LLOYD

Above: Two more pubs in Market Square – the Cross Keys and the Coach and Horses – stood together on its south-west side until the wholesale demolition of that side and all the properties behind it.

Right: The Harrow Inn, pictured in 1910, stood at the Cambridge Street end of Buckingham Street, with only a corner shop separating it from the older Barleycorn Inn round the corner. When the shop was demolished in the eighties, to give better traffic vision round the corner, the two Aylesbury Brewery pubs amalgamated and a new joint entrance was created on the corner.

Next page: Customers are lined up for an excursion from the seventeenth century Red Lion Inn in Kingsbury around 1910.

High Street, Aylesbury,

The Chandos Hotel, on the Exchange Street corner of High Street, was listed as the early headquarters of Aylesbury United Football Club. It is pictured around 1912 when its landlord, John Simmonds, doubled as a coal merchant at the LNWR station, across the road.

Near the station, at the lower end of Great Western Street, the 1898 Railway Hotel was an extravagant Victorian building complete with grotesque gargoyles. Described by Nikolaus Pevsner as 'an engaging little horror with a turret, gables and big blank arches,' it was bulldozed along with all its neighbours, shortly after 1964, when this photograph was taken.

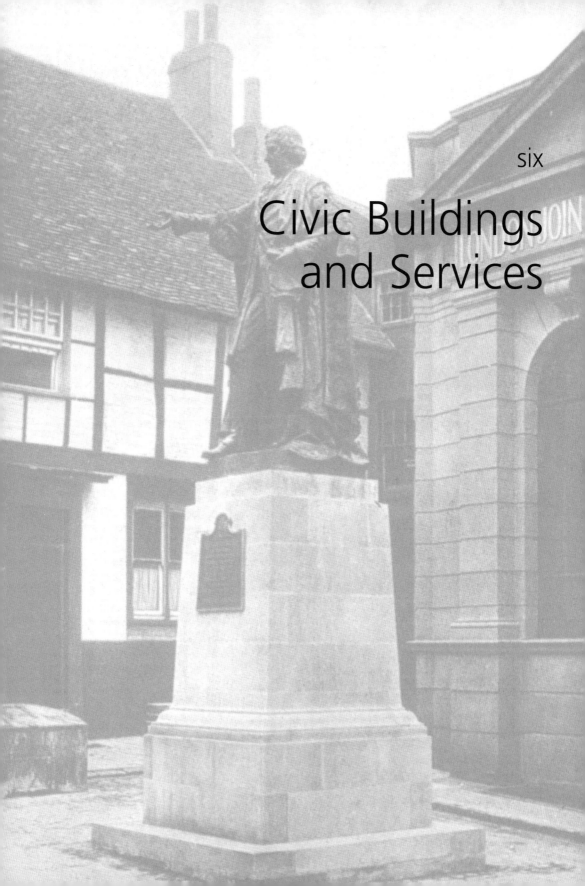

six

Civic Buildings and Services

Above left: This is one of a pair of docile-looking lions presented to the town in 1888 by Lord Rothschild. The cast-iron beasts had stood in his grounds at Waddesdon Manor before their final journey, steam-hauled along the road, to guard the County Hall.

Above right: This statue of Benjamin Disraeli, Earl of Beaconsfield, was unveiled in 1923 at the top of Market Square in the space beside The Crown.

Left: The foundation stone of the Clock Tower was laid in 1876 and the completed structure was handed over to the local council the following year. The illuminated clock had been presented to the town in 1857 by the lord of the manor, and was originally placed on the old Market House in the square.

Right and below: Buckinghamshire's most famous citizen, John Hampden the Patriot, whose refusal to pay the Ship Money demanded unlawfully by King Charles I helped to instigate the Civil War, is commemorated at the top of Market Square. His statue, locally said to be indicating the way to the public toilets behind the Corn Exchange arches, is officially showing his followers the route to his home at Great Hampden from the site of the Battle of Aylesbury which took place in 1642 just north of the town. On the plinth are two bas reliefs, portraying the battle of Chalgrove Field (pictured below) and the burial of Hampden, who was killed in that battle.

Another statue in Market Square is that of Major General Lord Chesham, who stands between the Rothschild lions at the lower end of Market Square, just across the road from County Hall.

Opposite above: When the Aylesbury Market Co. failed financially in 1901, the Urban District Council bought their Corn Exchange at a bargain price and converted it into the Town Hall, which hosted various civic functions, lectures, concerts, and entertainments including, in the early twenties, the Town Hall Kinema's 'carefully selected programmes' every Thursday and Friday at 6.00 p.m. and on Saturdays continuously from 3.30 p.m. The livestock market flourished in the area beyond the arches, and on this 1930 postcard three little pigs are trotting their way home, closely followed by the farmer.

Opposite below: Having completely filled County Hall and a later office block behind it, the county council erected this impressive building in 1928 around the corner in Walton Street and backing onto the existing offices. An additional wing was built in 1939, after which further expansion was carried out into houses on the opposite side of the road, beyond the shops as seen in this mid-1930s view.

COUNTY OFFICES AND WALTON STREET, AYLESBURY.   G.8902

This atmospheric view of the top of Market Square by lamplight dates from the late twenties. Aylesbury's War Memorial had been unveiled by the county's Lord Lieutenant on 15 September 1921 before a large crowd. The simple stone Cross of Sacrifice, bearing a bronze Crusader's Sword was modelled on those in the British war cemeteries in France. The tablets on the wall at the base of the cross bear the names of the Aylesbury residents who lost their lives in the First World War. Further tablets were unveiled in 1951 listing the victims of the Second World War.

The public swimming bath in Bourbon Street, mostly funded by the generosity of Baron Ferdinand Rothschild, was opened in 1895. The bath closed in 1939, superseded by the open-air bath at The Vale. The small building next door to the bath was the town's fire station.

After several years in shop premises in Bourbon Street and Temple Street, the main post office moved to its first purpose-built premises in High Street in 1889, when that street was still mainly residential. The solid-looking building, behind the lamp-post marking the entrance to the passage known as Hale Leys Square, on the right in this early twentieth-century view, served the town's postal needs until 1972, when a new building replaced it on the same site.

Three postmen are seen making their way through the snow in April 1908, beside the shops of lower High Street en route to the post office.

The County Infirmary opened in a large house at the corner of the Bicester and Buckingham Roads in 1833. It was rebuilt in 1862 to designs supervised by Florence Nightingale, sister-in-law of Sir Harry Verney, president of the management committee. The impressive building is pictured after the snowfall of April 1908.

The Verney ward for men is pictured in the early twenties. Citizens of Aylesbury could become hospital 'governors' for a subscription of two guineas per annum entitling them to nominate patients. These subscriptions, along with the proceeds of carnivals and street collections, etc., kept the hospital going.

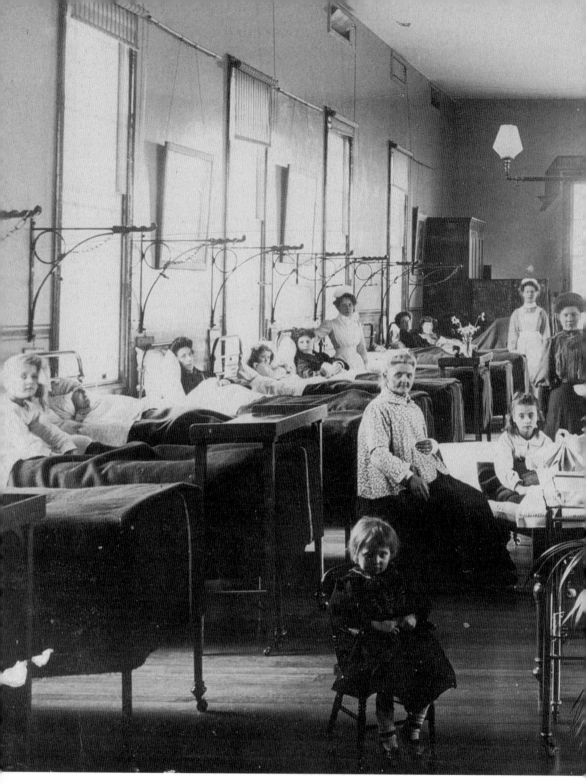

Seen here around 1915 is the Lee ward for women and children, in the west wing of the hospital, which by then had become known as the Royal Bucks.

In 1922 the Royal Bucks Hospital nurses' home was built on the opposite side of Bicester Road. It is pictured before extensions in 1926 and 1935 added another floor.

The Victoria Club for working men was erected on the corner of Kingsbury in 1887 by local MP, Lord Rothschild, to celebrate Her Majesty's Jubilee. The building offered a billiard room, reading room with a library of 400 volumes, lecture hall and refreshment bar, all for an annual subscription of 5s. It is pictured here from Buckingham Street looking along the top of Kingsbury around 1912.

The Voluntary Fire Brigade was supported by the local Board of Health and its successor, the Borough Council, who maintained the equipment and the fire station, until it became part of the National Fire Service in 1941. Here, in the twenties, the men proudly pose with their well-polished engines.

Aylesbury was the headquarters of the Buckinghamshire County Police Force, with the Chief Constable's office in Walton Street. Pictured in 1913, two mounted officers of the local force have found a quiet corner of Aylesbury during their routine patrol of the town.

In 1845 the county gaol in Aylesbury replaced that in Buckingham. Pictured in 1912, the entrance gates stand between the official residences of the governor and the chaplain. Initially, hard labour, when imposed, consisted of working a treadmill which pumped water for the few residents who could afford to pay for it. In 1877, the gaol became a female-convict prison, and a reformatory for inebriates was added in 1903.

St Mary's churchyard was closed for burials in 1855, and the following year the council established the cemetery on seven acres of land off Tring Road. Photographed from the road in 1907, with separate chapels for Anglicans (left) and Non-Conformists (right) behind the entrance gates, it had already been extended to ten acres. Further extensions around 1920 and 1933 doubled its size again.

Market Square was the town's first main shopping centre, and by the twenties several of the national multiples had moved in. The Victorian building at the centre of this 1920 postcard view had been occupied for over a decade by International Stores and Boots, with two local stationery businesses, Mark & Lee and Armstrong's, on the left.

Opposite above: At the bottom of Market Square, facing The Bell from the junction of Walton Street and Great Western Street was Arthur Samuels' Corner Shop, pictured here in a 1922 advertisement.

Opposite below: The whole area to the south west of Market Square, down the hill to the station, was demolished in the sixties and resulted in the loss of a network of small streets full of local character. The right side of Bourbon Street, looking toward Market Square, is a typical example of the variety of individual businesses in old buildings which were replaced by a concrete precinct containing branches of the same multiple stores as all other shopping centres.

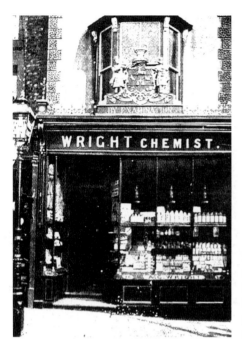

This is the decorative frontage of Arthur Wright's chemists on the north side of Market Square, pictured in 1907. As well as being a dispensing chemist, offering high-class pharmaceutical products, he stocked cameras, photographic apparatus, plates and papers, and had a darkroom available for customers' use.

Montague Burton's, the gents' outfitter and tailoring chain, built their Aylesbury shop in 1936 in the firm's standard style, with a billiard hall upstairs on the site of the former George Hotel. It was photographed from High Street a few years later.

Market Street, Aylesbury

Above: Pictured in 1930, George Margesson Adams' tobacconists shop at the top of Market Square, beside the entrance to Market Street, had been established for about ten years. He also ran a 'first-class hairdressing saloon' in Kingsbury, where he was also agent for leading shipping companies.

Right: Robert Whittaker, musical instrument and music dealer, seen here at the door of his Temple Street shop, used this card in 1908 to confirm a visit to a customer, a farmer at Dorton. The card, published in Tyneside, had been printed with the address AYLESBURGH, hence the over-printed correction.

Robert Whitaker, Piano and Music Warehouse
18, Temple St., ✳✳✳✳✳ Aylesbury

Kingsbury Square, Aylesbury.

Kingsbury, which was the first venue for the town's market, before Market Square took over that role, continued to offer a range of shops and services. The top (west) side is seen here in the mid-1920s, including (from left to right): a grocer's, The Rockwood pub, a basket maker's, a café, a butcher's, a printer's, and a car showroom. Just to the right of the ornamental drinking fountain is a captured First World War German tank, presented to the town in 1920 by the National War Savings Committee.

Walter Surfleet's chemists, near the Market Square end of Kingsbury, specialised in items for the sick room, stocking clinical thermometers, hot water bottles, inhalers, syringes, feeding cups, and bed pans in several sizes and designs. He also sold many varieties of natural mineral waters and health salts.

Aylesbury's longest established shop, already 180 years old when pictured in the early 1900s, was the family boot and shoe business in Kingsbury founded by Robert Ivatts. It continued through seven generations of the family, but was eventually sold in 1949, the end of an era which lasted 226 years.

Henry Sale made the picture frames he sold, together with furniture, at his Buckingham Street shop.
He is pictured in his woodworking apron on this 1900 card, on the back of which were advertisements:
'Nothing more suitable for a Christmas present than a nice picture', and 'Come and see my special show
of pictures at prices to suit all buyers'.

Cambridge Street was full of the little specialist shops seldom found in the main shopping streets. It
was pictured from outside the Barleycorn, and starts on the left with the 'back way' to the Harrow Inn,
around the corner in Buckingham Street.

Cambridge St & High St, Aylesbury.

Cambridge Street and High Street enter the top corner of Market Square with the round house, containing King & Sainsbury's tailors' shop, between them, all very busy with pedestrians in the early twenties. Before the opening to High Street was created in Victorian times, the Crown Hotel (extreme right) had been a much larger building, fronting onto the square.

The top end of High Street was pictured on a sunny day in the 1900s, with sun-blinds protecting the goods in all the south-facing shop windows. Starting from the right, the shops were: Hopcraft's confectionery, Jarvis' drapery, Stephens' millinery, Bishop's saddlery, Nelson's butchers, and clothiers the Target Stores.

Looking at some of the same High Street shops in 1961, the ladies' wear shop of Jarvis's, which extended through to Cambridge Street at the back of the block and recently expanded into the adjoining premises, had just started their summer sale which attracted large crowds.

This fifties view back toward Market Square shows some of the shops on the other side of High Street. Prominent is Spragg's outfitters, then James' fish and poultry stores and Fletcher's butchers shop, all established there for well over twenty years. Crown Buildings, the block of shops at the end of the street, occupies the site of the old Crown Hotel. The gleaming stone-work at the right edge of the picture is the doorway of the National Provincial Bank.

Further down High Street in the early 1900s, the café of Frank Richings, pastry cook and confectioner, on the left, bears the seemingly unlikely notice: 'Tents for Hire'. Next door, John Wood's chemists announced that they were official dispensers to the Royal Bucks Hospital.

Above and below: Frederick Longley, Aylesbury's first department store, opened in High Street around 1900, having started in a small way in Market Square some forty years earlier. Occupying the corner site at Britannia Street, Longley's provided accommodation for junior staff in adjacent buildings in both streets. In the late thirties the shop was demolished and replaced by Fifty Shilling Tailors. Later re-named John Collier, they remained on the corner until the 1980s.

High Street, Aylesbury

Further down High Street, looking back towards Longley's in the twenties, many of the buildings were still residential, while others had had shop fronts grafted on, over their original small gardens, for example Mills' outfitters and its immediate neighbours on the right and the isolated tobacconists shop on the left.

Walton, although within the Parish of Aylesbury, was once an entirely separate community with its own full selection of shops, including, near Walton Pond, the Walton Boot & Shoe Repairing Depot, pictured with the brothers who ran the business in 1918.

In addition to the main shopping streets, many Edwardian residential developments included small local shops, and a typical example of these, Harding's busy corner shop in Stoke Road beside the entrance to Chiltern Street, was pictured in about 1910.

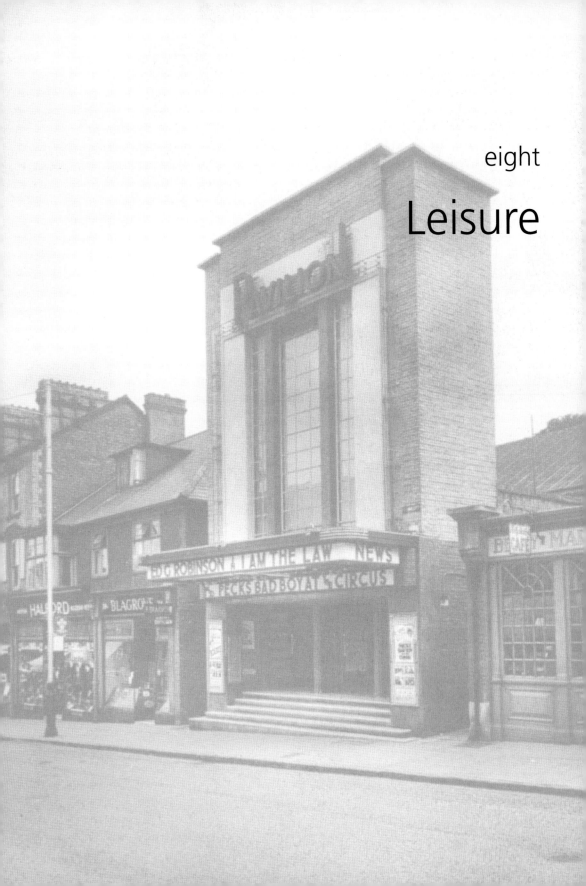

eight

Leisure

The Vale of Aylesbury Tennis Courts shared, with the cycling and athletics club, part of the open space which later became Vale Park. The area was bounded by High Street, the LNWR railway, Park Street (across the background of this 1906 postcard view) and the canal.

Vale of Aylesbury Tennis Court

Aylesbury Borough Council bought the land for Vale Park in 1929 and immediately laid out public tennis courts and a putting green, opened in May that year. The next phase was construction of the swimming bath adjacent to Park Street, which was opened in June 1935.

The new park also included two first-class bowling greens, the turf for which, according to the writer of this card, was brought from northern Scotland.

Near the High Street end of the park the council provided a small playground for children, equipped with see-saw, slide, various swings and a shallow paddling pool, pictured in the late thirties.

The completed Vale Park, with landscaped areas of grass, flowerbeds and ornamental trees, also shelters and seats for relaxation, was declared open in July 1937. Part of the well-laid out gardens is shown on this late forties postcard, with a backdrop of poplar trees hiding the industrial buildings.

Above: Noted for its chestnut trees, the Recreation Ground, between the cattle market and the buildings on the south side of High Street, had no playground or other facilities, but simply offered six acres of quiet open space near the heart of the town. Pictured in the early 1900s, the area was reduced by expansion of the market in 1927.

Left: Aylesbury's first purpose-designed cinema, the 1,000-seat Grand Pavilion in High Street, was built in 1925, by Mr Charles Senior, who had previously exhibited films at the Town Hall Kinema. Its title soon abbreviated to The Pavilion, the cinema was enlarged in 1936, and later became part of the Granada chain.

The Market Theatre, entered via a passage beside the Green Man Inn, was built behind the pub in 1911 as a music hall, belonging to the Aylesbury Electric Theatre Co. Doubling as theatre and cinema, when pictured, in 1921, it offered 'Varieties & Star Pictures' twice nightly, with programmes changing on Mondays and Thursdays and seat prices ranging from 5d to 2s.

Above: The town's second major cinema, The Odeon, in Cambridge Street, opened in June 1937 in direct competition with The Pavilion. The new building was photographed just prior to the opening, before tenants had been found for the integral shops, and with the façade carrying, instead of a film title, the message, 'Odeon extends a hearty welcome to Aylesbury'.

Left: In its early years, the Odeon published a monthly programme of forthcoming attractions. Illustrated with a sketch of the building, the pocket-sized folder did not include programme times, for which patrons were referred to the local papers. The films in this edition, issued during the Second World War, included the film *Target for Tonight,* described as an authentic story of a bombing raid on Germany, and *Philadelphia Story,* starring Katherine Hepburn, James Stewart and Cary Grant.

nine

Events

An annual feature of Aylesbury's social calendar was Lifeboat Saturday in June, when a procession around the town raised funds for the Royal National Lifeboat Institution. The 1906 event was a special one, with a real lifeboat 'borrowed' from Deal for the day – it is to be hoped that nobody needed help off the Kent coast while the boat was away. The boat was launched from its carriage on to the terminal basin of the canal before a good crowd of Aylesbury folk.

Opposite above: Aylesbury's celebrations of the postponed 1902 Coronation of King Edward VII omitted the usual public dinner as all the food had been bought before he was taken ill and had already been eaten. The proceedings included a procession of decorated carts and floats from the local Benefit Societies. The pictured float was entered by the Aylesbury & District branch of the National Deposit Friendly Society.

Opposite below: Church bazaars and fêtes were popular social occasions in the 1900s and this card, posted shortly afterwards, shows a very successful annual event, the Wesleyan bazaar which was open for two days in June 1904, during which the stall run by the sender of this card, took the sizeable sum of £460.

Above and below: Once afloat on the canal, the lifeboat gave short trips from the terminal basin as far as the High Street bridge, involving a difficult turn with such long oars in the narrow waterway there The usual parade also took place and included decorated bicycles, as photographed (below) by a local onlooker.

Above and below: In 1907 a squadron of Lancers, on manoeuvres, set up camp on the outskirts of Aylesbury. In the photograph above they are seen entering the town along the lower part of High Street. The lower photograph, one of a set of postcards depicting camp activities, shows the cook in his makeshift open-air kitchen under a corrugated iron roof beside a marquee, which was hired from its local maker, J. Putnam of Bicester Road.

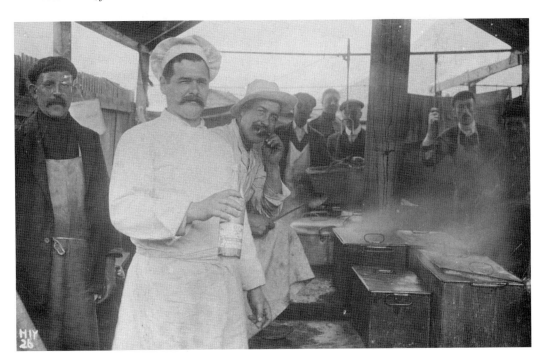

This page and opposite: Unseasonal weather in late April 1908, with snowfalls on both the 23rd and 26th, turned the most commonplace streets into photogenic scenes. Several of the town's photographers took advantage of the conditions and four of their pictures are seen on these pages: two road sweepers contemplating the vast area of snow in Market Square (above); while two more are clearing the pavement at the entrance to Kingsbury (below). The two views on page 111 are of Bicester Road.

Bicester Rd Aylesbury
23rd April 1908

Above and left: This statue of Maj.-Gen. Lord Chesham, between the Rothschild lions in front of County Hall, was unveiled on 14 July 1910 by Field Marshal Lord Roberts VC, under whom he had served during the Boer War. The pictures on this page show the Guard of Honour and some of the distinguished guests before the unveiling, and the unveiled statue with Lord Roberts saluting as he leaves the platform.

The final picture of the ceremony shows much of the crowd, both military and civilian, attending the event. The statue of the popular figure had been erected in his honour by a group of Lord Chesham's friends.

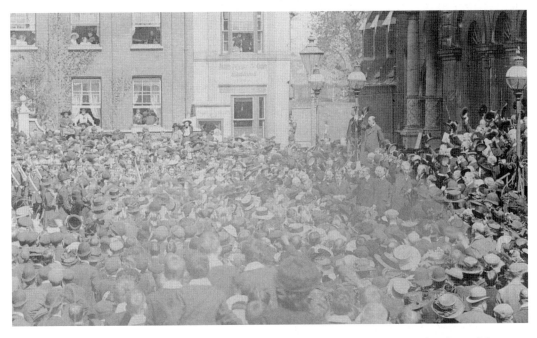

The proclamation of the accession of King George V was read before a large crowd in front of the town hall arches on 12 May 1910.

As part of the town's festivities to celebrate the Coronation of King George V on 22 June 1911, the foundation stone for the plinth to carry the John Hampden statue was laid in Market Square. A 'time capsule' of current local and national papers was deposited beneath the stone.

A year later, on 27 June 1912, the finished statue of John Hampden, which had already been exhibited at the Royal Academy, was unveiled by Lord Rothschild, the Lord Lieutenant of the County. The still-veiled statue is seen here, over the heads of the assembled crowd, in front of the George Hotel.

Right: This picture gives a clear view of the statue of John Hampden after the unveiling, with McIlroy's ironmongery showrooms and the crowded balcony of the George Hotel behind. The civic dignitaries are gathered closely around the plinth while the police hold back the general public.

Below: On 24 May 1913 a disastrous fire destroyed Gulliver's Wine Stores in Kingsbury and severely damaged several neighbouring buildings. A policeman and members of the Volunteer Fire Brigade pose with others involved, in front of the damaged buildings.

A major army exercise took place in the Aylesbury area in September 1913. This impressive line of traction engines, including a steam crane, together with a light car, a lorry and a Red Cross trailer, was part of the Ambulance Service Corps, also taking part in the exercise which was watched by senior military observers.

Opposite above: This relaxed contingent of men of the Bucks Hussars was on an exercise in the Aylesbury area in 1914 prior to embarking for the battlefields.

Opposite below: In October 1914 this group of soldiers from the north of England was billeted in Aylesbury. The men in the photograph were very new recruits, still in 'civvies', but the man who sent this card to his family in Durham had just been measured for his uniform.

Seen from behind the cross, this crowd, estimated at 5,000, occupying every available vantage point, assembled for the unveiling, by the Marquess of Lincolnshire, then Lord Lieutenant of Bucks, and the dedication ceremony of Aylesbury's War Memorial at the top of Market Square, on 15 September 1921.

In 1922 the local branches of the Women's Institute took part in a carnival parade which included Market Square in its processional route. The float, entered by the Ickford and Worminghall branch, stopped for the photographer outside Miss Armstrong's stationery shop.

This float, with all the participants advertising Horlicks, was entered in a charity parade in the mid-1920s. It represented the Aylesbury and Walton Sick Nursing Association, a charity which maintained two qualified nurses to assist the poor of the parishes with skilful nursing in their own homes for a subscription of 5s a year or 2s a visit, OAPs free.

HRH Princess Mary, Viscountess Lascelles, visited Aylesbury on 15 May 1926 to officially open the Girl Guides' Hall in Beaconsfield Road. She was presented with an illuminated address of welcome to the borough and, together with the County Guide commissioner, took the salute at a march past of local guides. This picture shows the saluting base in Walton Street.

On Saturday 2 November 1929, the Aylesbury United Friendly Society Appeals Committee organised a Torchlight Procession around the town to raise funds for the Royal Bucks Hospital. Preparing to take part, this donkey cart, hired from local dealer J. Smith, carries two 'Giant' figures, one of which is holding the newspaper-type programme for the event.

Opposite above: Circus proprietor, Bertram Mills, who was president of the Princes Risborough Show, organised a coaching marathon from Aylesbury to Princes Risborough in connection with the 1936 show. Here a well-laden coach is starting off from Market Square.

Opposite below: War Weapons Week in 1941 helped raise funds to pay for the armaments needed by the forces in the Second World War. Aylesbury's parade, on 19 April, included both military and civilian personnel, seen here marching down High Street past Bradford's and Robinson's on the north side of the street, where parking was then permitted on odd dates.

Above: To commemorate many years of friendly co-operation between Aylesbury and the RAF Technical Training Centre at nearby Halton, the men of Halton were granted the freedom of the borough in 1956. Here they are seen marching past the saluting base set up in front of county Hall.

Left: Exceptionally heavy rainfall in November 1954 resulted in considerable flooding in the lower parts of the town. Here, seen from the High Street gate, much of Vale Park was under several inches of water, with a raised flowerbed standing out as a square island.

ten

Schools

Aylesbury Grammar School was established around 1600 when a limited amount of teaching took place in a side-chapel of the parish church. A generous bequest provided for a school building in 1720 on the edge of St Mary's Square, beside Church Street, seen at the centre of this 1900 view from the churchyard. When the school moved to new buildings in 1907, the old school was taken over by the Buckinghamshire Archaeological Society and became the County Museum.

Grammar Schools, Aylesbury.

Above and below: Modern buildings funded by the Borough and County Councils were erected in Walton Road, and the new Aylesbury Grammar School was officially opened on 23 May 1907. A guide published during the building work noted that the 'thoroughly up-to-date secondary school' would have sanitary, well-lighted classrooms, art rooms, laboratory, dining rooms, warmed dressing rooms and excellent playing fields, together with a headmaster's house. The photographs of the building and of the school group in the grounds both date from 1913. Three years later the buildings were temporarily taken over as a military hospital.

Aylesbury Grammar School, 1913.

St Mary's Junior School was built in 1845 in Oxford Road to accommodate some 300 pupils. It was managed jointly with St John's School by a committee chaired by the vicar of St Mary's. The headmaster in the early twenties, Mr H. Smiter, is seen here to the right of the school football team.

In 1906 three council schools were built on a site between Kings Road and Queens Park, photographed here about ten years later. Officially opened on 30 April 1907, the buildings, which cost £12,000, catered for 390 boys, 350 girls, and 310 junior and infant pupils. Only two years later extensions were necessary, and in 1922 a fourth building, a woodwork centre, was added.

Right and below: This advertisement for Temple Square School appeared in a 1907 Aylesbury guide. Misses Amery and Gleaves had taken over the existing school around the turn of the century. Their 'Modern School for Girls' took both day and boarding pupils, with also a preparatory class for boys and a kindergarten. The group photograph of the school hockey club in 1909 includes, in the front row, Emily Gleaves, house mistress, and Annie Amery, headmistress.

Other local titles published by Tempus

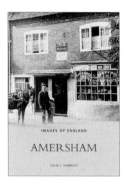

Amersham
COLIN J. SEABRIGHT

This absorbing collection of 190 old images recalls some of the important events that have occurred in the town of Amersham during the last 150 years, including the arrival of the railway in 1892. Aspects of everyday life are also featured, from shops and businesses, public houses and coaching inns, to sporting events, leisure pursuits and local townspeople.

0 7524 3245 1

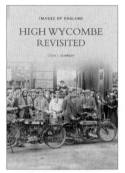

High Wycombe Revisited
COLIN J. SEABRIGHT

Alongside recollections of the area's industrial heritage this volume also recalls aspects of everyday life, from shops and public houses to leisure pursuits and celebrations. Illustrated with over 190 pictures *High Wycombe Revisited* recalls life in the town during the first half of the twentieth century, when much of the old town still remained.

0-7524-3678-3

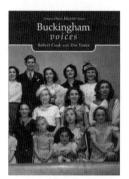

Buckingham Voices
ROBERT COOK WITH DES TUNKS

The town of Buckingham has seen many changes during the last century and it is the people, whose experiences and reminiscences are recorded here, who have shaped the area into the fascinating place it is today. This book brings together the personal memories of people who have lived and worked in Buckingham, vividly recalling childhood and schooldays, sport and leisure, the war years, and working life.

0 7524 2198 0

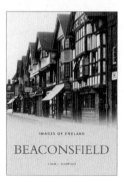

Beaconsfield
COLIN J. SEABRIGHT

This compilation of 200 archive images includes vistas of well-known streets like London Road, Warwick Road, Ledborough Lane and Penn Road, placed alongside images of shops, places of worship, schools and public houses, such as the oldest of Beaconsfield's many historic inns, The Royal Saracen's Head. This detailed and informative volume also records events, sporting activities, royal visits and local people who lived and worked in Beaconsfield over the last century.

0 7524 3093 9

If you are interested in purchasing other books published by Tempus, or in case you have difficulty finding any Tempus books in your local bookshop, you can also place orders directly through our website

www.tempus-publishing.com